GRADE **5**

PRACTICE READERS
VOLUME 1: UNITS 1 & 2

PEARSON

Glenview, Illinois • Boston, Massachusetts • Chandler, Arizona • Hoboken, New Jersey

PEARSON

ISBN-13: 978-0-328-79574-1
ISBN-10:   0-328-79574-7
4 5 6 7 8 9 10 V0B4 18 17 16 15

Table of Contents

Practice Reader 1A **1**
The Wreck of the *Edmund Fitzgerald*

Practice Passage 1B **5**
A Spring Day

Practice Passage 1C **7**
Growing Tomatoes from Seeds

Practice Reader 2A **9**
Career Advice

Practice Passage 2B **13**
Sir Nigel and the Dragon

Practice Passage 2C **15**
Town Needs New School

Practice Reader 3A **17**
Gramma's Cornbread

Practice Passage 3B **21**
A Tour of a Landmark

Practice Passage 3C **23**
Summertime

Practice Reader 4A. **25**
Charlotte Brontë and Jane Eyre

Practice Passage 4B **29**
A Musical Time Capsule

Practice Passage 4C **31**
A Sport Called Wiff-Waff

Practice Reader 5A. **33**
Sending News from Camp

Practice Passage 5B **37**
Tornado Warning!

Practice Passage 5C **39**
Packing a Suitcase

Practice Reader 6A. **41**
The Nation's Capital City

Practice Passage 6B **45**
Called to Order

Practice Passage 6C **47**
The Pilgrims

Practice Reader 7A. **49**
In the Keys

Practice Passage 7B **53**
It's Grand

Practice Passage 7C **55**
West

Practice Reader 8A **57**
A Day at the Opera

Practice Passage 8B **61**
A Place of Pesky Insects

Practice Passage 8C **63**
Henri Matisse

Practice Reader 9A **65**
A Prime Number

Practice Passage 9B **69**
The Taj Mahal

Practice Passage 9C **71**
The Best Place in the World

Practice Reader 10A **73**
The Life of a Cowboy

Practice Passage 10B **77**
A Pueblo Market

Practice Passage 10C **79**
A Fiesta in Bueno

Practice Reader 11A **81**
America's First Sport

Practice Passage 11B **85**
It's Magnetic

Practice Passage 11C **87**
Assembly Line

Practice Reader 12A **89**
Amazing Amazonia

Practice Passage 12B **93**
Pluto a Mini-planet

Practice Passage 12C **95**
The Tale of the Silent Cheetah

Practice Reader 13A **97**
Helping Burn Victims Heal

Practice Passage 13B **101**
Down by the River

Practice Passage 13C **103**
Daisy the Dinosaur

Practice Reader 14A **105**
The Alarm

Practice Passage 14B **109**
A Pirate's Wreck

Practice Passage 14C **111**
One Woman's High Jump

Practice Reader 15A **113**
Whale Watching

Practice Passage 15B **117**
Arthur Ashe, Tennis Champion

Practice Passage 15C **119**
American Buffalo

Practice Reader 16A **121**
Curiosity and the Tree

Practice Passage 16B **125**
Whistles, Bells, and Steamboats

Practice Passage 16C **127**
It's Sticky Stuff

Practice Reader 17A **129**
Garden Fun

Practice Passage 17B **133**
Crazy Apply Salad

Practice Passage 17C **135**
The Surprise Visitor

Practice Reader 18A **137**
Paul and Other Octopuses

Practice Passage 18B **141**
Ötzi the Cook

Practice Passage 18C **143**
Pets and the President

The Wreck of the *Edmund Fitzgerald*

by Bruce Gordon

The SS *Edmund Fitzgerald* was over 700 feet long.

Suffix *-ly*

abruptly	exactly	suddenly
certainly	really	unexpectedly
clearly	slowly	unfortunately
completely		

1

On November 10, 1975, the *Edmund Fitzgerald,* a Great Lakes freighter, sank in Lake Superior. All 29 men on board were killed. No one knows exactly why the ship sank. But certainly a ferocious storm was the main factor.

The *Fitzgerald* was carrying taconite, an ore, from Superior, Wisconsin, to Zug Island near Detroit, Michigan. When the ship left on the afternoon of November 9, her captain, Ernest M. McSorley, knew that a storm was coming. But that was not unusual for November on Lake Superior, and McSorley was an experienced captain. Unfortunately, this storm proved to be one of the worst ever seen on the lake.

The National Weather Service issued first gale warnings and then storm warnings. Later, the Coast Guard closed the locks at Sault St. Marie and urged all ships to seek safe anchorage. The storm was bringing hurricane-force winds and massive waves, some as high as 35 feet, to the lake.

Messages between the *Fitzgerald* and other ships in the area showed that the *Fitzgerald* was having some problems because of damage from the storm. But nothing indicated that those problems were serious enough to really threaten the ship. However, the *Arthur M. Anderson,* a ship that was traveling with the *Fitzgerald,* had its last communication with the other ship at 7:10 P.M. The *Fitzgerald* then disappeared completely off the radar. Worried, the *Anderson's* captain reported his concern to the Coast Guard.

The Coast Guard asked the *Anderson* and any other ships in the area to look for the *Fitzgerald*. They found some debris, but that was all. Later, wreckage was discovered 530 feet deep 17 miles off Whitefish Point, Michigan. The bow and the stern lay in separate sections. The name *Edmund Fitzgerald* could be seen clearly on the stern.

The Great Lakes Shipwreck Museum displays the bell from the *Edmund Fitzgerald*.

Why did the ship sink so suddenly and unexpectedly? Why were there no distress signals? Why didn't the men launch any lifeboats? One theory is that the high waves poured water onto the ore. Slowly the ore became heavier and the ship rode lower in the water. Then when a huge wave hit the ship, its bow went down and could not come back up. The ship plunged abruptly into the lake. The crew never had a chance.

A Spring Day

by Flora Diaz

Suffix -ly

briefly	patiently	steadily
brightly	quickly	strongly
gently	really	suddenly
happily	repeatedly	warmly
loudly	slowly	

On this beautiful spring day, the sun shone brightly, and a breeze blew warmly and gently. It was such a contrast to the gloomy skies and cold temperatures of the weeks before. People flocked to the park to enjoy being outside in the nice weather. Some played ball on the grass and threw sticks for their dogs to catch. Some jogged and skated up and down the paths. Others lounged on the benches, turning their pale faces toward the sun.

Small children squealed happily as they tossed bread crumbs to the ducks in the pond and rode around and around on the antique carousel. It played the same three tunes repeatedly and loudly, but no one cared on this day. Many people waited patiently in long lines to buy ice cream cones and cold drinks from the vendors while others wandered slowly past the beds of tulips and other spring flowers whose colors dazzled the eyes.

A few small clouds drifted into the clear blue sky. Then more clouds appeared. Suddenly the sky was more gray than blue, and the breeze started to blow more strongly. Now it did not feel so warm or gentle, and people began to drift away. The clouds darkened steadily, and in the distance, lightning flashed briefly and thunder rumbled. As the first raindrops fell, people moved more quickly. Some hurried home, and others headed into shops and restaurants. Within minutes, it was raining really hard, and the ducks had the whole park to themselves.

Growing Tomatoes from Seeds

by the Garden Guru

Suffix *-ly*

carefully	impatiently	regularly
evenly	loosely	safely
finally	proudly	thoroughly
firmly	really	truly
gently		

Are you waiting impatiently to get your garden going? Do you wonder if winter will ever truly be over? While you are waiting and wondering, why not start growing tomatoes from seeds? Begin in March and by June you will have plenty of sturdy seedlings ready to plant outside in your garden.

1. Fill small flowerpots with fresh potting soil.
2. Press the soil until it is firmly packed.
3. Sprinkle a few tomato seeds evenly on top of the soil.
4. Put a little soil in another pot and shake it gently over the seeds.
5. Cover the pot loosely with plastic wrap. Hold the plastic wrap in place with a rubber band.
6. Put the pots in a warm place until the seeds begin to sprout.
7. Carefully move the seedlings to their own pots.
8. When the weather gets really warm, you can safely plant the seedlings outside.
9. Put a tomato cage around each plant. Remember, tomatoes are heavy, so the plants will need some strong support.
10. Weed around the plants regularly and check for bugs.
11. Water the plants thoroughly and give them plant food once a week.

Finally, prepare to enjoy juicy, delicious tomatoes all summer and to proudly share them with friends and neighbors.

Career Advice

by James Bradley

Greek and Latin Roots

archaeologists	dentists	predict
astronomers	geologists	protect
biology	include	pursue
botanists	photographer	zoologists

Have you considered what career you will pursue in the future? Do the possibilities seem wonderful but endless? You will find it helpful if you try to narrow down your choices, and one way to do this is to think about your interests. What do you like to do?

Do you enjoy discovering new things? If so, then perhaps you will want to be a scientist. Although all scientists have much in common, there are many kinds of science and scientists.

For example, biology is the study of living things. Biologists include zoologists, who study animals, and botanists, who study plants. Other scientists are geologists, who study the earth, and astronomers, who study the sun, moon, planets, stars, and so on. Archaeologists study people and life in the past to figure out how we got where we are now while meteorologists study the weather and try to predict what will happen in the future. Whatever subject you are interested in, there are likely scientists studying it, and you could be one of them.

Are you interested in helping people? Then maybe you will want to be a physician. Some doctors are general practitioners who treat all kinds of problems; other doctors are specialists who focus on one area of the body, such as the brain, the digestive system, or the eyes. Dentists take care of people's teeth.

Other careers that involve helping people are police officers, who protect people, enforce laws, and solve crimes, and firefighters, who put out fires and help in emergencies. Teachers and professors help students learn what they need to know to become successful citizens and workers.

Are you more interested in helping animals? You might become a veterinarian, or animal doctor. Some veterinarians specialize in large animals, such as horses and cows, while others specialize in small animals, such as cats and dogs. Zoo veterinarians work with more exotic animals, such as elephants and lions.

Do you enjoy being creative? Do you like to write stories, paint, play an instrument, or take pictures? Then you might want to consider a career as a writer, artist, musician, or photographer. In any event, keep creating now because who knows what may come out of that later.

Yes, the options are limitless, but don't let that scare you. First, focus on developing your own interests and then later look for connections between them and possible careers.

Sir Nigel and the Dragon

by Leslie DeRamus

Greek and Latin Roots

accepted	continued	reluctant
agreed	delighted	surprised
botanist	protect	zoologist
confided	pursuit	

Once upon a time, in a faraway kingdom none of us will ever see, there lived a ferocious dragon. In accepted dragon tradition, he breathed fire, stole cattle, and generally terrorized the people of the kingdom. The king sent knight after knight to fight the dragon, but none ever returned and the dragon continued to wreak havoc. Finally, the king sent Sir Nigel.

Nigel was a reluctant knight. He really wanted to be a zoologist and study animals rather than kill them. Still, he had sworn to protect the people of the kingdom, so he rode out in pursuit of the dragon.

After exchanging numerous threats and blows, Nigel and the dragon grew weary. They decided to stop for tea. The dragon (whose name was Fred) confided that he was a reluctant marauder. He really wanted to be a botanist and study plants. Nigel and the dragon worked out a treaty. The dragon agreed to stop breathing fire, purchase his own cattle, and leave the people of the kingdom alone if the king would stop sending knights to try to kill him. Nigel took the treaty back to the king, who frankly was surprised to see him but delighted to sign the treaty. Fred the dragon went on to become a famous botanist who discovered a rare plant, which he named *flora nigelus* in honor of Nigel. Nigel, a knight no more, became a famous zoologist who discovered an unusual animal, which he named *reptilus freda* in honor of the dragon. And everyone lived happily ever after.

Town Needs New School

by the *Belleville Gazette*

Greek and Latin Roots

auditorium	effective	require
benefit	expensive	succeed
computer	reconstruction	sympathize
democracy		

Citizens of Belleville: We need a new elementary school now. That is the issue, plain and simple. Our current school is a century old. It has been in our town for as long as there has been a town, and we sympathize with those who think of it as a beloved landmark. However, despite careful maintenance and constant upgrades, the school has not been able to keep up with the times. We must face the fact that it is time for a new school.

Our children need more classrooms and more and better computer and science labs. They need a bigger, better-equipped gym and a modern auditorium that can double as a theater or concert hall. Our young scholars, scientists, athletes, actors, and musicians will only benefit from these changes. Then there are the safety issues. A school should have a sprinkler system and secure entrances, but our beautiful old school does not.

It is impossible to add all these features to the old school. Its electrical and plumbing systems are outdated and already overburdened, and replacing those systems would be too expensive. The present layout would require major reconstruction. It is simply more cost effective to make a fresh start.

Let's give our children the facilities they need to succeed in the twenty-first century. On April 8 vote yes for a new school. Remember, in a democracy, every vote counts, so be sure to cast your ballot.

Gramma's Cornbread

by Kathleen Theroux

Compound Words

anything	granddaughter	tablespoons
buttermilk	grandmother	teaspoons
cookbook	headache	toothpick
cornbread	lifetime	worktable
corncobs	notebook	worthwhile
cornmeal	someday	

What can I say about my grandmother's cornbread? It's simply the best cornbread in the world. She didn't get the recipe from a cookbook, though. She says her cornbread came about through lots of trial and error over the course of a lifetime. Now she is teaching me how to make it!

17

First, we gather all the ingredients we'll need on the big worktable in Gramma's kitchen. Most of the ingredients are what you'd expect in cornbread—flour, cornmeal, salt, baking powder, baking soda, sugar, eggs, milk, shortening. Some are different. Instead of milk, Gramma uses buttermilk. She uses fresh corn as well as cornmeal. We scrape the kernels and juice off the corncobs, which is a terribly messy but ultimately worthwhile chore. Also, Gramma uses a mixture of whole wheat flour and all-purpose flour. Some people use butter; Gramma, a true southerner, uses shortening.

Next we mix the ingredients. Dry ingredients—flour, cornmeal, salt, baking powder, baking soda, sugar—go in one bowl. "Wet" ingredients—eggs, buttermilk, shortening, fresh corn kernels and juice—go in another bowl. That step would be easy to do except for one thing: Gramma doesn't measure anything. No cups, no tablespoons, no teaspoons for her, no sirree. Instead she puts in about this much of that, a handful or so of this, a pinch of that, maybe a dash more, stir, hmm, now a little more of this. I try to watch what she is doing *and* write details about the steps in my notebook. I get a headache.

Then we add the dry ingredients to the wet ingredients, a little at a time, and stir them together. Gramma lets the batter sit for a while so it can "breathe," she says. When she is satisfied with how the batter looks and feels, she pours it into a hot cast-iron skillet (no baking pans for her) and puts it into the preheated oven. She can tell me the temperature, but not the amount of time. She says the only way to tell if the cornbread is done is to stick a toothpick in the middle and see if it comes out clean.

It may take me a while, all right, it may take me years, but I vow that someday I'll be making cornbread as good as Gramma's and teaching my granddaughter how to make it.

A Tour of a Landmark

by the Franklin County Historical Society

Compound Words

armchairs	driveway	rooftop
backyard	fireplace	rosebushes
bathroom	greenhouse	showpiece
bathtub	hallway	staircase
bedrooms	handcrafted	storeroom
bookcases	hometown	sundown
businessman	horsehair	sunup
downstairs	landmark	upstairs
downtown	outside	wallpaper

Welcome to the Detwiler Historic Home, an important Franklin landmark. Herman J. Detwiler arrived in 1868 and opened the first general store downtown. For years he worked from sunup to sundown, living in a storeroom at the back before building this house in 1885 to show his success as a businessman.

We are standing in the downstairs hallway, which runs from the front door to the back door. There are two rooms on either side of the hallway—parlor and study on the right, dining room and kitchen on the left. Note the evidence of Mr. Detwiler's prosperity: The parlor has an elaborate fireplace mantel and wallpaper while the study has floor-to-ceiling mahogany bookcases and horsehair armchairs imported from England.

As we climb the staircase, note the handcrafted banisters. There are four bedrooms upstairs, two rooms on either side of the hallway. And here at the back is the showpiece of the house and Mr. Detwiler's pride and joy: a bathroom with an ornate bathtub imported from France.

Let's go back downstairs and outside to the backyard. In 1888 Mr. Detwiler married Matilda Hochstadt, who came from his hometown in Pennsylvania. These rosebushes were Mrs. Detwiler's pride and joy, and she had this greenhouse built so the family could have fruits and vegetables all year.

On your way out, pause on the driveway and look up at the weather vane on the rooftop. It is in the shape of a large D for Detwiler. Thank you for visiting the Detwiler Historic Home.

Summertime

by Tomas Alvarez

Compound Words

airplane	outdoor	snowstorms
baseball	outside	summertime
basketball	popcorn	sunburned
drawback	rainfall	sunscreen
fireworks	seafood	sunshine
football	seashells	swimsuit
grandparents	seashore	weekend
jellyfish		

It's easy to name my favorite time of year: summertime! I mean, what's *not* to like about it? The weather is hot and sunny. In fact, there's so much sunshine that you have to put on sunscreen so you won't get sunburned, but that's a small price to pay for great weather.

I get to do all my favorite activities in the summertime. I can put on a swimsuit and go swimming every day. I can play basketball outside with my friends. I can watch fireworks by the lake every weekend and read books the way I eat popcorn: as many and as quickly as I want.

Every summer my family boards an airplane and flies to Mexico to visit my grandparents, who live in a big house on the seashore. We walk on the beach and collect unusual seashells, we listen to my grandparents tell stories about their childhoods, and we go into town and eat delicious seafood. There *is* one drawback: When you go swimming in the ocean, you have to watch out for jellyfish because they can sting you.

Do I miss spring's rainfall or winter's snowstorms? No, I'd rather have sun and heat than rain or snow. Do I miss fall's football? Well, okay, maybe I miss that a little, but in the summer I can watch baseball games instead.

Summer has wonderful weather, fun outdoor activities, and a trip to Mexico. Is it any wonder that I like summertime best?

Charlotte Brontë and *Jane Eyre*

by Susan Temple

The home where Charlotte Brontë lived in Haworth, England, is now a museum.

Shades of Meaning

admired, loved	cried, uttered	injustice, unfairness
bully, mistreated	freedom, liberty	
content, happy	high-strung, sensitive	popular, respected

25

Jane Eyre, the title character of the novel *Jane Eyre*, published in 1847, is one of the most popular fictional characters of all time. Jane is intelligent and sensitive. She is polite but refuses to give in to unfairness. Another aspect of Jane's popularity is her resemblance to her creator, Charlotte Brontë. The lives of both Charlotte and her character show some problems of children and women in England in the 1800s.

In the novel, Jane Eyre, an orphan, lives in England with her uncle's family. After Jane's uncle dies, Mrs. Reed and her children bully Jane and treat her disrespectfully.

Mrs. Reed sends Jane to a boarding school, but Jane is mistreated there also. She and the other girls are not given enough to eat, and they are always cold. Many girls get sick, and Jane's best friend dies. After this tragedy the school gets new management, and the girls' lives improve. After Jane completes her education there, she teaches at the school for two years.

Charlotte Brontë's vivid descriptions of Jane's boarding school sadden and anger readers. However, they called readers' attention to the problems of schools like Jane's that existed at the time.

Charlotte's childhood was similar in some ways to that of her character. Although Charlotte Brontë was not an orphan, her mother died when she was young. It was hard for her father, a minister, to raise Charlotte and her five siblings after their mother died. Charlotte's aunt came to care for the family, but she was not warm and loving. Like Jane Eyre, Charlotte and three of her sisters were sent away to a boarding school that made many girls ill. After Charlotte's two older sisters passed away, Charlotte and her younger sister Emily were sent home.

In England in the 1800s, women had few ways to make a living. Most women were not allowed to become doctors or lawyers or own businesses. Charlotte's fictional character, Jane, longs for the freedom to earn a living and be treated with respect. She becomes a governess, like many real women in her position. Soon she is content, teaching a little girl for a wealthy, mysterious man, Mr. Rochester.

Charlotte Brontë published *Jane Eyre* in 1847.

Charlotte, like Jane, had limited ways to earn a living. Perhaps because of the many tragedies she had suffered, she was high-strung during some times in her life. She became a private teacher for a while and then tried to open her own school with her sisters. However, the school was not successful.

The novel *Jane Eyre* has a happy ending. Charlotte Brontë also became happy when she devoted herself to writing. She wrote four novels, and the second one, *Jane Eyre,* became a huge success. Readers and critics loved Jane and admired Charlotte's ability to portray women's lives. Many women could identify with Jane when she cried: "For liberty I gasped; for liberty I uttered a prayer." Today, *Jane Eyre* gives readers a striking picture of life in the 1800s. It reminds them of the limited opportunities women had. It shows readers the importance of self-respect and of fighting injustice.

In *Jane Eyre,* Jane becomes an independent woman and later is happily married. Charlotte Brontë also got married, but died soon after, at the age of 39. But her remarkable character Jane Eyre has made Charlotte Brontë one of the most respected writers in English literature.

A Musical Time Capsule

by Janice Tate

Shades of Meaning

glanced, looking, scrutinizing	headed, rushed	pile, stack	tossing, passing, pitching

Jacob usually didn't get bored, but this Sunday afternoon, when he and his mom were visiting Granddad, was an exception. Normally, Jacob and Granddad would be tossing a football, passing a basketball, or pitching a baseball; but recent knee surgery had temporarily sidelined Granddad.

"Why don't you go down to the basement and check out my arrowhead collection?" Granddad said. Jacob had seen the Native American arrowheads many times, but he headed downstairs, hoping to find something he hadn't explored. As he glanced around the room, a foot-high pile in a corner caught his eye. It was a stack of record albums, their covers splashed with colorful photos and artwork: awesome!

Scrutinizing Granddad's music, Jacob found many rock albums from the 1970s and '80s—and here was a Beatles album from 1966! Now, if only there was a turntable; at least Jacob recognized that was a necessity for playing records. There it was: a small turntable hooked up to a couple of speakers.

After Jacob carefully put the Beatles album on the spindle and pressed *On*, the record dropped to the turntable, and the long arm with the needle floated to the outer edge of the record. This machine sure did have a lot of moving parts! The cheerful sound of the Beatles, with lively electric guitars and smooth vocal harmonies, poured into the room.

Looking through the album covers, Jacob discovered some jazz and classical titles. Jacob heard Mom calling and rushed upstairs; those records could wait for another boring Sunday.

A Sport Called Wiff-Waff

Henry Roberts

Shades of Meaning

competitors, players	knock, strike	pastime, sport
easy, simple	made, produced	

What sport can be played in your basement or at the Olympic Games? What sport is played on a table and has been nicknamed "wiff-waff"? It's table tennis, of course!

Table tennis began in the 1880s as a pastime for British military officers in India. They brought the game home to England. At first, the "net" was a row of books. The paddle could be a book or a hard box lid. The ball could be a golf ball or a cork.

As the game became more popular, commercial toy makers began to make table tennis equipment. The first rackets made especially for the game were made of parchment on a frame. In 1901, a British table tennis player found balls in the United States made of celluloid, a light plastic. They were perfect for table tennis. In the same year, paddles like those used today were produced. They had wooden frames with bumpy rubber covers.

The rules of table tennis are simple. After the serve, you must return the ball after no more than one bounce on your side of the net. The first player to score 11 points wins. If the players are tied at 10, the winner must win by two points. Each player serves twice and then his or her opponent serves twice. If you can knock a table tennis ball across the net, you may think the game is easy. But the best table tennis competitors strike the ball with amazing power. They give the ball a tricky spin. Both singles and doubles table tennis competitions became official Olympic sports in 1988.

Sending News from Camp

by Ana Ortiz

Inflected Ending -ing

aching	frightening	sailing
amazing	gathering	saying
being	getting	seeing
betting	going	sending
biking	gripping	showing
canoeing	hanging	signing
climbing	having	singing
coming	hiking	starring
considering	hoping	staying
creating	interesting	sticking
decorating	letting	swimming
diving	loving	swinging
doing	making	taking
expecting	meeting	telling
feeling	performing	thinking
fencing	planning	trying
finding	predicting	worrying
fishing	repeating	wrapping
flattering	riding	writing

Dear Mom and Dad,

    You probably weren't expecting to hear from me so soon, but I've been staying at camp for three days now, and I'm letting you know so you won't be worrying about me: This place is *great!*

    There are so many interesting things to do here. Just for kicks, I'm betting that I can go five days in a row without repeating an activity! Here's what I've been doing so far.

    The first day I went horseback riding and I tried canoeing. My legs and arms are still aching from all that saddle gripping and paddle swinging, but I had a good time and I'm planning to do both again.

    Yesterday I went swimming in the lake and hiking in the woods. Tomorrow I'm going rock climbing in the mountains. The camp is certainly in a beautiful location, with a lake, woods, and mountains all right here.

Today I went fishing for the first time ever and I caught a good-sized trout! Ben, my counselor, said I was showing signs of having a knack for fishing. This afternoon I'm taking a crafts class in which we'll be making and decorating small leather bags. So someone may be getting one of these as a gift in the future!

As I said, I'm going rock climbing tomorrow, and I'm also signing up for archery. I'm hoping that my legs and arms hold out! For the last day of my five-day plan, I'm considering mountain biking and fencing. Then I will go back to the activities I liked best. I'm thinking that fishing will definitely be on the list!

Every night after dinner you will see us gathering outside the main lodge in the middle of the camp for all-camp activities. Cabins take turns singing songs, telling stories, and performing skits. My cabin is really good at telling stories that are both funny and frightening. Right now we're creating a skit to perform tomorrow night. I'm predicting it will be the best skit of the entire summer. Of course, I may be biased since I have the starring role in the skit.

My seven cabinmates are awesome, and I'm not saying that because they chose me to be the star in our skit! Two are from New York, two are from California, and the others are from Puerto Rico, Florida, and Canada. They are an amazing group. You should see Lena diving from the high board. I watch her with my mouth hanging open. Carrie is the one who should be showing me how to ride. She rides in competitions. Emma has been sailing since she was two years old, so she is an expert. Grace, a terrific photographer, has been taking so many pictures of us. Some are flattering, some not so much, such as one of me with my hair sticking out in all directions! Mia is always coming up with the funniest jokes, Claire does most of our writing, and Siobhan is clever at finding whatever we need for our projects.

So, as you can see, I'm meeting new people, making new friends, trying new activities, and having a wonderful time.

Well, it's lights out now, so I must be wrapping this up. Thanks again for letting me go to camp. I know you were feeling nervous about my being away from home for a month, but I'm fine and I'll be seeing you soon.

Your loving daughter,
Ana

Tornado Warning!

by Jason Hess

Inflected Ending *-ing*

beeping	receiving	threatening
depending	rotating	wailing
happening	spinning	warning
heading	staying	watching
occurring		

Tornadoes can happen when cold, wet air from the Arctic meets with warm air from the Gulf of Mexico and dry air from the Rocky Mountains. These rotating air masses can have wind speeds of more than 200 miles per hour! A wildly spinning tornado can rip trees out of the ground, pick up cars and toss them several feet, and destroy buildings. Because tornadoes can be so destructive, there are warning systems that help save lives.

The severe weather season can last from March to November, depending on where you live. Meteorologists spend this time watching for changes in temperature, rain, and wind patterns. When a tornado seems likely, the National Weather Service lets people know about it. Then they can find a safe place to shelter from the storm. You may hear a siren wailing outside or an alarm beeping on television. A message will tell you where the tornado is heading; it will also tell you what you can do to stay safe.

The National Weather Service gives different messages based on what is happening. A *tornado watch* means that a thunderstorm could happen, but there may or may not be a tornado. A *tornado warning* means that a tornado is either occurring or about to occur. Anyone in an area receiving a tornado warning should take cover right away. Staying out in the open can be very dangerous. It can even be life threatening.

Packing a Suitcase

by Amelia McCrae

Inflected Ending *-ing*

doing	making	screening
dragging	overpacking	slipping
dropping	packing	sorting
facing	placing	stuffing
folding	planning	taking
going	putting	using
lifting	rolling	

Are you tired of dragging an overstuffed suitcase on your trips? Is your suitcase so heavy that you have trouble lifting it off the floor, much less putting it into an overhead bin? Believe it or not, packing a lighter suitcase is easy to do, and I'm going to show you how.

First, I have gathered all the items I'm planning to take on my trip. Now I'm taking out half of them! That's the only way to avoid overpacking. Focus on making every item work in more than one way.

Never take more than three pairs of shoes. Wear one pair and pack the other two. I'm slipping each shoe into a resealable bag or plastic grocery bag and placing the shoes around the outer edge of my suitcase, with the soles facing out.

Now I'm sorting my clothing items by weight. Heavier items go on the bottom; lighter items go on top of them. Some people swear by rolling; others claim folding uses space better. Whichever way you use, once all these items are in the suitcase, you should be stuffing smaller things, such as socks and underwear, into the leftover spaces around the bigger items. See what I'm doing? I'm using every bit of available space.

Last, I'm dropping my bag of toiletries on top. That way I can get it out quickly for security screening at the airport. I'm packed and ready to go, and I've got a suitcase that I can handle easily.

The Nation's Capital City

by Tanya Elliot

The Lincoln Memorial was built in the early 1900s and opened to the public in 1922.

Homographs and Homonyms

addresses	close	stairs
capital	sight	stares
capitol	site	

Washington, D.C., our nation's capital city, is a great place to visit. Visitors can spend days enjoying the city's many historic government buildings, memorials, and museums.

You may want to begin your city tour on Capitol Hill. Here you can visit the domed Capitol. The Capitol is where the Senate and the House of Representatives meet. It is also the site where American Presidents take the oath of office and give their inaugural addresses. Other important buildings on the Hill are the Supreme Court Building and the Library of Congress.

Look west across the National Mall, and the tallest sight you will see is the Washington Monument. This monument, standing a little more than 555 feet (169 meters), is a memorial to George Washington. It is also the city's tallest building.

Lining the National Mall are many of the nation's great museums. Here you will find the Smithsonian Museums. These include the National Portrait Gallery, the National Air and Space Museum, the National Gallery of Art, and National Museum of Natural History.

At the far west end of the Mall, a building stands in honor of Abraham Lincoln. This is the impressive Lincoln Memorial. The Lincoln Memorial is open 24 hours a day. It does not close. You can visit it night or day.

The outside of the monument has thirty-six columns. Each column represents one of the states that were part of the nation when Lincoln was President. The inside of the monument has three sections. In the middle section, an enormous statue of Lincoln stares out across the Mall. In 1963, Martin Luther King Jr. stood on one of the stairs of the monument and delivered his famous "I have a Dream" speech.

Close to the Lincoln Memorial is the Vietnam Veterans Memorial. The granite walls of this memorial list the names of Americans who died or were missing in the Vietnam War.

North of the Mall is Pennsylvania Avenue. The National Archives is located on this street. The Archives is home to the nation's most important documents. The Constitution, Bill of Rights, and Declaration of Independence can be seen here.

John Adams, our second President, was the first President to live in the White House.

One of the best-known addresses on the street is 1600 Pennsylvania. This is the location of the White House, the home of the President and his family.

From the White House to the museums and memorials to the National Archives, our national capital has much to offer all visitors. Whatever your interests, you are sure to find many wonderful places to visit and explore in Washington, D.C.

Called to Order

by Ana Lara

Homographs and Homonyms

conduct	minute(s)	principal
council	object	principle
counsel		

"This meeting of the Brent City Council is now called to order." These or similar words open official meetings of city councils around the nation. A city council is the governing body of a local community. In many communities, a mayor is the city official who presides over the council meetings.

In most meetings, the first order of business is to approve the minutes from the previous meeting. The minutes are meeting notes. The minutes include only the most important ideas discussed, not unimportant or minute details.

During a meeting, council members discuss issues affecting the community as well as proposed new rules. Sometimes members disagree on issues or proposed rules. Some members may support a proposed rule while others object to it. Most city councils have city attorneys who provide legal counsel. The advice of the attorney can help the members of a council make decisions. After discussion, council members may vote on a proposed rule. If more members vote for the rule than against it, the rule becomes a law.

At some meetings, the council may allow public comment. The object of the public comment period is for citizens to express their views on issues important to the community.

Many communities conduct their meetings based on the *Robert's Rules of Order.* The principal purpose of *Robert's Rules* is to ensure that every meeting runs smoothly. When the principles and procedures outlined in the Rules are followed, meetings are orderly and participant's conduct is appropriately respectful. This enables a council to efficiently and effectively conduct the business of its community.

The Pilgrims

by Michael Paisley

Homographs and Homonyms

compact	peace	right
knew	piece	write
new		

The Pilgrims wanted to live in peace and practice their religion freely. To gain this freedom, they looked to the Americas. In September 1620, the Pilgrims boarded the *Mayflower* and went to sea. The small, compact ship was filled with 102 passengers and their goods.

The ocean crossing was difficult, and the ship did not land in the right place. The Pilgrims were sailing for Virginia, but they landed in New England. Although the Pilgrims knew they were in the wrong region, they chose to stay where they were. They then looked for a good piece of land for their new home. They found it at Plymouth.

Before they left the ship, however, the Pilgrim leaders decided to write an agreement for forming a government. That agreement was called the Mayflower Compact. The Pilgrims agreed to create a government with just and fair laws. The forty-one men aboard the ship signed the agreement. Today, the Mayflower Compact is considered an important step in the founding of the American democracy.

The Pilgrims were able to set up a successful colony in Plymouth. Their survival, however, depended on Native Americans. The Native Americans taught the Pilgrims how to hunt and fish and how to grow American corn, squash, and beans. Together the Pilgrims and Native Americans agreed to treaties that enabled the Pilgrims to live in peace.

In the Keys

by Elsa Mumford

The National Key Deer Refuge was established to protect the wildlife and plants of the Florida Keys.

Words from Spanish

alligators	hurricane	manatees
Florida	iguanas	mosquito
hammock	Keys	

When Mom first said we were going to Florida for vacation, I was excited. I saw myself enjoying rides in theme parks.

"You must have misunderstood," Mom said, dashing my dreams. "We are going to Florida, but we're going to the Florida Keys." The Keys are a chain of islands that curve southwest around the southern coast of Florida.

The Keys have long been connected to the mainland of Florida at first by a railroad and then by a highway. In the early 1900s a railroad could take passengers from Miami all the way to Key West. Key West is the island farthest away from the coast of mainland Florida. However, the railroad was destroyed in 1935 when an enormous hurricane struck the Keys. It was never rebuilt. Today an overseas highway links the Keys to the mainland.

When vacation time came, Mom, Grandpa, and I armed ourselves with sunscreen and mosquito repellent and flew to Miami. We rented a car there and drove along the overseas highway from Miami to our destination, Big Pine Key.

Big Pine Key is one of the southernmost keys. Grandpa said that as soon as we got there, he was going to hang a hammock between two trees and spend the entire time relaxing. Mom had other ideas for our vacation. She is an animal lover and a hiker, so her plan was to spend the two weeks enjoying nature. You can guess whose plans we followed.

Mom was thrilled as we drove through the Keys because we saw iguanas everywhere. These lizards are not native to Florida, but like many people, they now call it home.

When we arrived at Big Pine Key, I was amazed. We saw the tiniest deer roaming through the area. Big Pine Key is the home of the National Key Deer Refuge. The refuge has pine forests, wetlands, and forests of mangrove trees. The refuge was set up to protect the tiny key deer that were once in danger of extinction. Today the deer thrive. The deer in the refuge are not afraid of humans. They will come near people, but we were told not to touch or feed them.

One day we went to an old rock quarry called Blue Hole. Filled with water, Blue Hole and its surroundings make a good habitat for many animals including alligators. We even saw alligators lounging in the sun there. Imagine that! We actually saw alligators in the wild!

On another excursion, we took a boat trip around the Keys and saw a group of manatees. Also called, sea cows, manatees are large, odd-looking animals. Many older manatees have scars from being hit by motorboats. Now Florida has laws to protect them.

Our two weeks at Big Pine flew by. As we were packing to drive back to Miami and fly home, I turned to Mom and told her that this was the best trip ever. "The Florida Keys are nature's theme park." Grandpa agreed.

It's Grand

by Shelby Reynolds

Words from Spanish

burro   Colorado   ranch

canyon

Though I'm not particularly adventurous, I couldn't imagine visiting the Grand Canyon without riding a burro to the floor of the canyon. My friend chuckled and informed me that mules, not burros, are the animals used to descend into the canyon. Once we got that settled, we made our plans for my first visit to the Grand Canyon.

We researched information about the mule rides, thinking that we would ride to the canyon floor and stay overnight at a ranch there. The ranch is close to the Colorado River that carved the Grand Canyon millions of years ago. We decided that with my lack of riding experience, we probably were not up to that challenge. We opted for a shorter ride to the Abyss Overlook instead.

This was my first trip to the canyon, and I was one excited tourist. When we drove into the Grand Canyon National Park, we stopped at vantage points along the road. I can't begin to describe the grandeur of the canyon. It is awe-inspiring. The first day there we walked along the rim. Every view was breathtaking. Pictures do not do the canyon justice.

I was looking forward to the mule ride and was a bit nervous, but I shouldn't have been. The mules are well-trained, sure-footed, gentle animals. We rode them through forests to the Abyss Overlook, where we saw grand vistas of pinnacles and mesas.

I hope to revisit the canyon again and again, and on the next trip, I just might take that mule trip to the canyon floor.

West

by Cal Monsano

Words from Spanish

broncos	lasso	rodeo
chaps	mustangs	stampedes
lariat	ranch	

"You have the perfect name for a rodeo performer!"
West Franklin heard that comment a lot. People saw his
name on a program, and their minds immediately flashed
to the Old West and cowhand lore.

West didn't mind the association. He had grown
up on a Texas ranch founded by his great-great-
grandparents. The family told tales of the early years
when cowhands drove the cattle along the cattle trails to
market. He heard of stampedes that scattered the cattle
and endangered the cowhands. He heard stories about
catching mustangs and busting the broncos. The Old
West was part of West's family history.

The family ranch is where West learned to ride and rope. He got his first pair of chaps and a bandanna when he was six. He learned to ride on a gentle nag. Then he graduated to a spirited steed. He practiced throwing a lariat at a bucket for months and months before he ever tried to lasso a calf.

West began competing in the junior rodeo when he was in sixth grade. Later he joined the rodeo circuit and became a champion. He was the proud owner of gold and silver belt buckles. West's rodeo skills set him on the path to a new career. He was asked to do riding stunts for a movie. This led to other roles. Before long, West hung up his chaps and became a film star. Yet, the Old West still calls to him. When it does, he returns to the family's ranch, where he's teaching his own son to rope a bucket.

A Day at the Opera

by Luisa Sepulveda

English Words from French

ballet	clichés	program
boulevard	costumes	rapport
chandeliers	foyer	

Olivia was looking forward to the weekend: her Aunt Alicia had invited her to go somewhere special. Her aunt hadn't said where exactly. Olivia was hoping for the new movie about werewolves or maybe a huge shopping spree. Olivia and Aunt Alicia had a special rapport, and they had enjoyed a wide variety of activities together.

Olivia was dressed in her favorite turquoise jacket when her aunt arrived on Saturday. "I'm taking you somewhere you've never been before, Olivia. We're going to the opera!"

"The opera—but that's just a bunch of people singing in very deep or incredibly high voices about things that nobody understands!"

Aunt Alicia, laughing, said, "Those are clichés, Olivia. You enjoyed going to the ballet and to the musical *Annie.* The opera is a form of musical theater with great costumes, wonderful drama, and unbelievable live music."

For the first time in her life, Olivia was dubious about an activity Aunt Alicia had chosen. As she and her aunt boarded the train and rode into the city, Aunt Alicia gave her a preview. "It's a German opera, *Hansel and Gretel,* by a composer with a funny name: Engelbert Humperdinck."

This was sounding worse all the time. A fairy tale in German by Humperbert Engeldinck? "How will we understand it if it's in German?"

"The theater actually shows subtitles in English above the stage. I promise you'll love it!"

Olivia and her aunt left the train, walked a few blocks, and crossed a wide boulevard. Olivia was impressed as they entered the enormous opera house. Atop the high-ceilinged foyer, crystal chandeliers glittered over a crowd of chattering people.

Engelbert Humperdinck wrote the opera *Hansel and Gretel* in the 1890s.

As they reached their seats and the orchestra tuned their instruments, Olivia had to admit that she felt excited. When the lights dimmed and the opera began, Olivia forgot to feel surprised at her enjoyment. She lost herself in the dramatization of the familiar fairy tale: the children in their peasant clothes, the dark spooky woods, and the truly frightening witch. The singers' voices ranged from high sopranos to deep baritones. They sounded clear and thrilling in the big theater.

During intermission, Olivia read her program carefully. She was curious about the history of this opera and other ones the company would be presenting that season. After the opera's finale, Olivia felt slightly melancholy. The play had had a happy ending, but she was sorry to leave the enchanted world she'd lived in for a while.

On the train back home, Aunt Alicia asked Olivia what she was thinking about. "I'm wondering what opera I should see next. I'm considering *Madama Butterfly* or *The Magic Flute*."

A Place of Pesky Insects

by Lucille Brunin

English Words from French

armoire	decorative	porcelain
cuisines	objet d'art	

Have you ever gone to a flea market with your family on a Saturday or Sunday? If so, you know the thrill of looking for an unrecognized treasure or a unique objet d'art.

Who would want to buy or sell fleas, anyway? The name of these markets is not literal, of course. It probably came from a market held in Paris, France, in the 1860s. The market was called the French term for "flea market" because of the annoying insects that lived in some of the old sofas for sale.

One of the first flea markets in America took place in Texas in the 1870s. People came to buy and sell horses every Monday and soon brought other goods to sell too. In Connecticut in the 1950s, an antiques seller invited antique dealers to sell their merchandise outdoors. Soon people came to sell all kinds of "stuff," not just antiques.

Today, antiques dealers know that they can sometimes find treasures at flea markets. But they use certain guidelines. For example, they get to the market early. The early bird really does get the best antiques. Also, they focus on one or two specific items. They might look for antique clocks or porcelain. Then they learn all about these items, so that they recognize a valuable item when they discover one.

It really is possible to find a priceless piece of art, furniture, or decorative accessory at a flea market. But whether you find a valuable antique armoire in which to store your clothes or just sample some delicious cuisines at food stands, you will probably be entertained there.

Henri Matisse

by Shel Thompson

English Words from French

bouquets	debut	maroons
collages	Impressionism	pastel

The late 1800s was an important time in the French art world. Painters had created a new style called Impressionism. These artists wanted to be different. They focused on creating color, light, and movement. For example, Claude Monet created a series of paintings of haystacks. Each one showed the haystacks from a different angle at a different time of day.

The French artist Henri Matisse was born in 1869. He planned to become a lawyer. At the age of 20, he was recovering from a serious illness. His mother brought him paints and brushes, and soon he had become an artist.

Matisse began by painting in the traditional French style. But then a teacher introduced him to art by Impressionist painters. Soon he was using colors more creatively. For example, *Woman with a Hat* shows a woman with yellow cheeks. The painting includes a range of shades from pastel pinks to dark maroons. He painted his still lifes of fruit and bouquets in vibrant colors. After his debut art show in 1904, someone who did not like his work said, "A pot of paint has been flung in the face of the public."

Soon Matisse met another painter who did not follow old rules: Pablo Picasso. They became friends, and their art showed some similarities. In the 1940s and '50s, Matisse created a series of colorful collages. They were made out of bright, simple paper shapes. He also designed stained-glass windows. Since his death in 1954, Matisse has gained fame as a pioneer of modern art.

A Prime Number

by Pat Holcomb

Jackie Robinson helped integrate baseball's major leagues when he was hired to play for the Brooklyn Dodgers in the late 1940s.

-tion and *-ion*

appreciation	contribution	recognition
associations	distinction	segregation
complications	obstructions	separation
confusion		

If you were to go to a Major League Baseball game on April 15, there might be confusion about which player on the field was which. That's because all the players wear the number 42 on April 15 each year. Why 42? It's the number worn by Jackie Robinson, one of the most influential baseball players ever. Players wear number 42 in recognition of Robinson's contribution to baseball and the nation.

Baseball has been "America's Pastime" since the late 1800s. In the country professional teams formed associations called leagues. In the 1940s, there were 16 professional baseball teams in the American and National Leagues. But no African Americans played in the major leagues. African Americans played in a separate league called the Negro League. In the 1950s, African Americans did not have all the rights of other Americans. For example, in the Southern states, they were not welcome at some restaurants and hotels.

Branch Rickey was the general manager of the Brooklyn Dodgers baseball team. In 1945 Rickey decided it was time to end segregation in baseball. He saw no reason for the separation of players into leagues based on race. He invited Jackie Robinson to join the Montreal Royals, a minor league team in the Brooklyn organization. Robinson had played baseball, basketball, and football and had run track at UCLA. In 1945 he was playing for the Kansas City Monarchs in the Negro League.

Rickey and Robinson both knew that there would be complications for the first African American Major League Baseball player. Robinson would face prejudice from fans, the opposition teams, and even his own teammates. But Robinson decided to seize this opportunity. He would play baseball with the best players in the country and perhaps change attitudes toward racial equality.

Jackie Robinson heads for first base during a World Series game in 1955.

Robinson faced obstructions but also admiration, especially from African American fans. He proved that he was a fine player, with a batting average of .297 and 12 home runs in his first major league season. He led the league in stolen bases. His skills in the field as first baseman and later as second baseman were solid. He was named MLB Rookie of the Year. Robinson's skills and calm disposition won over his teammates, baseball fans, and opposing players. In 1949, Robinson played with distinction and was elected Most Valuable Player of the National League. He went on to play ten seasons for the Brooklyn Dodgers.

After his baseball career, Robinson continued to fight for rights for African Americans. Unfortunately, Robinson died when he was only 53. He was awarded the Presidential Medal of Freedom and Congressional Gold Medal after his death.

Starting in 2004, Major League Baseball made April 15 Jackie Robinson Day. All Major League Baseball players wear special shirts with the number 42. They show their appreciation for a courageous man who helped changed not only Major League Baseball but America itself.

The Taj Mahal

by Reese Bourmas

-tion and -ion

construction	decorations	expression
creation	dedication	reflection

What construction or building do you consider civilization's greatest? The United States has the Washington Monument and the Statue of Liberty. Egypt has the great pyramids. India has an amazing monument, the Taj Mahal, which some call the most beautiful building in the world.

From 1526 until 1757, the Mughal emperors reigned in India. During their reign, the kingdom experienced peace and harmony as well as economic and cultural growth. The fifth emperor of the Mughal Empire was Shah Jahan, who oversaw the Golden Age of arts in the empire. Inspired by Islamic, Persian, Turkish, and Indian architecture, the Mughal people designed impressive buildings throughout India.

The Taj Mahal was created because of a touching though tragic love story. Shah Jahan was heartbroken when his wife died in 1631. The building of a monument to his wife began in 1632 and was completed in 1653. The main part of the structure is a tomb with an arched doorway and a dome. The round *onion dome* is considered the most magnificent part of the monument. It is topped by a gilded finial. Four minarets are situated at the four angles of the tomb. In front of the tomb, a pool provides an other-wordly reflection of the monument.

The Taj Mahal is made of white marble with many intricate and colorful decorations. It appears to change colors throughout the day, glowing pink at sunrise and yellow and orange at sunset. If you get to see this spectacular creation someday, remember how Shah Jahan described the experience: "The sight of this mansion creates sorrowing sighs; And the sun and the moon shed tears from their eyes." The Taj Mahal remains a symbol of the shah's dedication to his wife and a magnificent expression of everlasting love.

The Best Place in the World

by Tanya Corwin

-tion and -ion

construction	emotions	fascination
dejection	exhilaration	introduction
elation	expression	

Libby and her family lived in a suburb of Washington, D.C., and she loved it. She enjoyed school field trips to government buildings and museums. She enjoyed spring's cherry blossoms and winter's snow-covered hills. Libby considered it the best place in the world. Then one day Libby returned from school and was surprised to see her dad already home.

"I've got exciting news, Libby," Dad said. "The Navy is transferring me, and we're moving to San Diego, California." Libby's expression revealed her emotions. This was the most unwelcome, unexciting news ever.

On the family's long trip southwest, Libby couldn't enjoy the extraordinary scenery. She could only focus on her dejection. She was leaving the best place in the world. Libby experienced no exhilaration on glimpsing the palm trees and open spaces of San Diego. The family's new house was a flat, whitewashed construction. It was nothing like their substantial red brick house on the East Coast.

Libby stood in her new front yard, wondering how long her family might be exiled on the West Coast. Then an athletic-looking girl strode across the street toward her. "Hi, my name's Serena, and I want to welcome you to San Diego."

Libby appreciated her neighbor's introduction. She responded, "Be honest! Do you like it here?"

Serena looked at Libby in fascination. "We go to the beach constantly. We have barbecues and play soccer outdoors all year. Seriously, San Diego's the best place in the universe."

Libby had to smile at Serena's elation. She'd try to like San Diego—and hope that someday she'd call it the second best place in the world.

The Life of a Cowboy

by the Cimarron Historical Society

Words from Spanish

arroyos	lariat	rodeos
canyons	lasso	stampedes
chaps	mesquite	tornadoes
corrals	ranch	vaqueros

The golden age of the cowboy lasted only about twenty years, from 1867 to 1886. After the Civil War, there was an expanding market for beef in the North and East. Texans began gathering cattle that had thrived on the open range. They moved the cattle to railheads to be shipped to other parts of the country. The men who helped move these herds were known originally as vaqueros, drovers, or herders. Later, they were called cowboys.

Twice a year cowboys rounded up the cattle on the open range. In the spring they branded the young cattle with the rancher's mark. In the fall they drove the cattle to the nearest railroad, often hundreds of miles away. A herd of cattle could travel only about 15 miles a day, so a cattle drive could take many weeks.

A nineteenth-century cowboy's life was hard and dangerous. He worked from sunup to sundown every day. He was out in all kinds of weather from blazing heat to bitter cold. He was almost always on horseback. He slept outside on the ground and ate the same foods day after day. He endured droughts, lightning, tornadoes, wild animals, and stampedes. He faced all that for about a dollar a day plus food and a bed in a bunkhouse if he was at a ranch and not out on the range or the trail.

Plus, it was seasonal work, lasting only from spring to fall. Most cowboys had to find other work in the winter. They also tended to move from ranch to ranch each year.

It was a job for young, healthy, strong, unmarried men who knew horses and cattle, wanted to work outdoors, and did not expect to get rich.

Often the cowboys who drove cattle were not the same as the cowboys who worked on the ranches. Besides roundups, a ranch cowboy's jobs might include moving cattle to and from winter or summer pastures and searching for stray cattle in canyons and arroyos. He would also build and mend fences and corrals and cut hay and grass to feed the cattle.

Much of a cowboy's clothing and equipment came from the clothing and equipment of the vaqueros. Every item was practical and purposeful.

Next to his horses (he had more than one), a cowboy's most important possession was his saddle. After all, he spent many hours every day sitting on it. A cowboy also needed a lariat, a rope of rawhide or hemp. He would lasso cattle with the lariat and then tie it to the pommel or horn of his saddle. A wide-brimmed hat protected his head from sun and rain. Leather chaps protected his legs from mesquite and other thorny brush.

A cowboy wore a bandana or kerchief around his neck to pull over his mouth and nose. This was very useful when following cattle herds that raised huge clouds of dust. He wore boots with heels because they stayed better in the stirrups of his saddle.

Rodeos also grew out of the traditions of the vaqueros. They would show off their skills at annual roundups. At the end of cattle drives, cowboys would have friendly competitions to see who was the best rider or roper. Later, many cowboys made their livings riding and roping in rodeo events. By then, railroad cattle cars had replaced cattle drives. Barbed wire had divided up the open range. The era of the cowboy was over. However, the influence of the cowboy lives on, even today more than 125 years later.

A Pueblo Market

by Lauren Gillespie

Words from Spanish

adobe	chilies	papayas
avocados	cilantro	potatoes
bananas	guacamole	pueblo
canyons	mesas	tomatoes

This farmers' market is a photographer's dream, and I found it completely by accident, but that's often how the best things happen. I have been exploring the land of mesas and canyons. I was wandering around this pueblo, admiring the adobe buildings, when I came across the market.

I have never seen fruits and vegetables in so many colors, shapes, and sizes. Everywhere I look, there is a scene that would make a wonderful photograph. It is so amazing that I hardly know where to start!

Here a table is piled high with brown, white, red, purple, and black potatoes, all thrown together higgledy-piggledy. There a stand is filled with tomatoes, carefully arranged by size—large, medium, small, tiny—and color—red, orange, pink, green striped. Fat strings of red and green chilies hang all over the front and sides of this booth. Piles of yellow, red, and brown bananas nestle up next to stacks of golden-orange papayas and melons of many kinds. I can see stacks of limes, oranges, and pomelos in that stand. And over there are onions and corn and lettuce—the list goes on and on.

Oh, my gosh, look at all the avocados, every one of them a beauty! Wait a minute, avocados, tomatoes, onions, and limes. Hey, if I can find salt and cilantro, I'll have all the ingredients I need to make guacamole! What a delicious treat that will be, but photographs first, treats second. Let's start with that table of multicolored potatoes.

A Fiesta in Bueno

by Aaron Fine

Words From Spanish

adobe	enchiladas	pronto
barbecued	fiesta	tacos
breeze	Florida	tamales
California	plaza	

The Acostas were driving from Florida to California. This had seemed like an excellent idea when they set out in the family car four days ago. But after another long day on the road, this one spent crossing miles and miles of desert, they were happy to come to the town of Bueno. They parked the car and got out to stretch their legs and explore.

A cluster of old adobe buildings surrounded a large plaza in the center of the town. Tall trees in the plaza provided welcome shade. But better yet, a fiesta was taking place there.

The smell of barbecued beef wafted on the breeze and made Mr. Acosta's mouth water. He followed the smell to its source: one of a number of booths that were selling food. Suddenly breakfast seemed a long, long time ago, and the Acostas couldn't think of anything besides eating lunch pronto.

They decided that each family member would choose one food for their meal. Mr. Acosta chose the barbecue that had first attracted him. Mrs. Acosta chose tamales, Lucio chose tacos, and Reina chose enchiladas. They gathered on a bench to share and enjoy their feast. Everything was fresh and homemade. It all tasted so good. And in ten minutes, it was all gone. After taking a brisk stroll around the town, the Acostas got back in their car and on the road, declaring that Bueno (which is Spanish for "good") was indeed *bueno*.

America's First Sport

by Grace Hampton

BALL-PLAYING ON THE PRAIRIES.

Native Americans invented the game of lacrosse.

Word Families

opposing/
opposition

organizations/
organized/
unorganized

popular/popularity

regulated/
regulations

standard/
standardized

81

Lacrosse is fast becoming one of the most popular games in America, but it certainly isn't new. In fact, Lacrosse is considered to be America's first sport. Native Americans invented the game of stickball centuries ago.

Different versions of the game were played by different groups of Native Americans. For the Iroquois, the game was a physical challenge, requiring great speed and skill, and a tribute to the gods. Each player on the team had a stick with a net on one end. The net was used to scoop, catch, and throw a ball. Balls were made of stone, bone, wood, deerskin, or baked clay.

Rules didn't dictate the number of players for a team, so hundreds of players might be on each team. Because there were few rules and no standard field sizes, the games were very unorganized. Play was rough and injuries were common. Played in the open plains between villages, games could last for days. Legend has it that the goals were sometimes a mile or more apart with no side boundaries and games lasted several days.

A game began with the ball being tossed into the air. The two sides then rushed to catch it. Teams scored points by hitting their team's goal with the ball. The goals were trees or large rocks. Players on one team ran with the ball in their nets. Players on the opposing team tried to steal the ball from the opposition. When a player reached the team's goal, he threw the ball at it.

In the 1800s French settlers in Canada became interested in the game and tried to make the game more organized. They regulated the size of the teams and the playing field. They also named the game *la crosse,* French words meaning "the stick." In 1867, a Canadian named W. George Beers standardized the rules of the game. The popularity of the sport spread quickly throughout Canada and the United States.

Today the game is played in North America, Europe, and Australia. National and international organizations promote lacrosse as a sport. The game is now played with two teams of ten players. Players line up on the field based on the positions they play, and they must stay in certain parts of the field depending on their positions. The goals are large nets about six feet high and six feet wide. The playing field is about the size of a soccer field. The ball is made of rubber and all equipment is made according to official regulations.

Modern lacrosse has its roots in the game played by the Native Americans, but teams now play according to standard rules. When the game was first played, only men played. Today boys and girls of all ages play lacrosse. Lacrosse is still an important part of Native American culture too. Today like others, Native Americans play lacrosse for fun and competition. Yet many Native Americans still consider it a spiritual and healing sport.

It's Magnetic

by Teresa Olivas

Word Families

attract/attraction

investigated/
investigation

magnet/magnetic/
nonmagnetic

metal/metallic/
nonmetallic

observation/
observe

science/scientific

Perhaps you have used a magnet to attach a picture to your refrigerator. You have likely investigated magnets and their properties in science class. Magnets have two poles, a south pole and a north pole. The magnetic field is strongest at the polar regions. You can make a scientific observation of the magnetic field by sprinkling iron shavings over a bar magnet covered by a sheet of paper. You will observe that more shavings are arranged near the ends of the magnets. This is where the poles are located.

In your investigation of magnets, you can use two magnets to observe how opposite poles attract one another and like poles repel. The attraction of the south pole of one magnet to the north pole of another magnet pulls them together. Two like poles repel each other. If you place the south poles of two magnets together, they will push apart. The same thing happens when two north poles are placed together.

Iron, cobalt, and nickel are three magnetic metals. Most steel, an alloy, or mixture, of iron and other metallic and nonmetallic substances, is magnetic. However, you may have noticed that magnets do not hold notes to a stainless steel refrigerator. Stainless steel is nonmagnetic. Aluminum and copper are two other nonmagnetic metals.

Magnets have many uses other than posting artwork on refrigerators. Magnets are an important part of today's technology. They are found in televisions, computers, and headphones. Medical equipment such as magnetic resonance imaging use magnets. Magnets are an important part of our everyday modern lives.

Assembly Line

by Ben Samuels

Word Families

afford/affordable

assembling/assembly

industrial/industry

introduced/introduction

invent/invention

produced/production

repeat/repetition

The automobile industry began after the invention of a gas-powered engine in the late 1800s. Before long car companies became industrial giants. One of the best-known early carmakers was Henry Ford. Ford did not invent the automobile, but he produced the first affordable car, the Model T. Before Ford introduced the Model T, only the wealthy could afford to buy cars. The first Model Ts were expensive. They cost more than $800, but over time the price dropped. The last Model Ts sold for about $300.

How could Ford produce such low-cost cars? He developed a moving assembly line. Workers stood in place putting the car together as parts moved by them. Each worker added parts to the car as it moved along the line. This way of assembling cars saved time. Now workers could build a car in less than two hours.

The introduction of the moving assembly line did have some drawbacks. Workers had to repeat the same task over and over again. Workers used to go from station to station, performing different tasks. This repetition kept them in one place. Standing in one place doing the same task was hard for many workers. Some left Ford to work at other plants. To encourage workers to stay at the Ford plant, the company began paying them $5 a day. This was more than workers could earn anywhere else. The pay raise kept workers on the line.

The production methods used to build the Model T made it possible for workers not only to build the Model T but also to own one.

Amazing Amazonia

by Enrico Vargas

Endings -s, -ed, -ing

adapted	exposed	layered
attacking	farming	reaching
being	floods	receives
burned	flowing	seeps
dropping	growing	threatened
eating	including	towering
estimated		

Orchids are growing from the trunk of trees. Colorful parrots are eating nuts and fruits. These exotic plants and animals live in the Amazon Rain Forest in South America. Also called Amazonia, the Amazon Rain Forest is the world's largest tropical rain forest. It spans northern Brazil and parts of seven other countries. Flowing into and through the rain forest is the Amazon River, the world's second longest river, and its tributaries.

Amazonia is warm and wet. Its average temperature is about 80° Fahrenheit (27° Celsius). In some regions, the rain forest receives about 300 inches (762 centimeters) or more of rain each year. Other areas are dryer and may get less than 100 inches (254 centimeters) of rain a year. Every year the Amazon floods over the land in the summer months.

Amazonia, like other rain forests, is a layered ecosystem with four layers. Different plants and animals are adapted to live in the layers. Towering high above the other layers is the emergent layer. The tall trees are exposed to wind, sun, and rain. The trees in this layer have waxy leaves. Birds, monkeys, snakes, and insects live in this layer.

Below the emergent level is the canopy. The canopy trees are very leafy, and they block much of the sunlight from reaching lower levels. Most of the plant and animal life of the rain forest is found in the canopy. It is estimated that 60 to 90 percent of life in the rain forest is found here. Here is where orchids and many other plants, such as ferns and mosses, grow on the trunks of trees. Many different animals live in the canopy, eating seeds and fruits. Monkeys, birds including parrots, and sloths are among the inhabitants of this layer.

Below the canopy is the understory. Here smaller trees grow. The trees have large leaves to gather the sunlight that seeps through the canopy. This layer has many tree frogs, lizards, snakes, and insects. The lowest level is the forest floor. Few plants grow here, but fallen leaves, branches, and fruit are decaying here. Worms and termites live in this layer. Larger animals live here too. Jaguars live and hunt on the forest floor, but as tree climbers, they may use the trees of the understory as perches for dropping down and attacking prey. Capybaras, the world's biggest rodents, turtles, and anteaters also live here.

The Amazon River system also has a rich variety of animal life. One of the most beautiful inhabitants of the river is the Amazon pink river dolphin. Giant river otters swim in the waters of the Amazon. Piranhas also live in the river. These fish with very sharp teeth swarm together as they feed on other animals in the river. Anacondas, large snakes of the rain forest, live near the river.

The Amazon Rain Forest has a great diversity of life, but the forest is threatened. Every year trees are cut for lumber or burned to clear the land for farming. Today efforts are being made to preserve the forest and its richness of life.

Pluto: A Mini-planet

by Luisa Alvarez

Endings -s, -ed, -ing

circling	hoping	predicted
classified	interested	reclassified
detected	looking	studying
discovered	named	suggested
honors	orbited	using

For many years, scientists knew about only eight planets in the solar system. Then in the early 1900s, astronomer Percival Lowell predicted that a ninth planet orbited the sun, and he began looking for it. Lowell did not find it, but in 1930, Clyde W. Tombaugh detected Pluto. Using a powerful telescope and photographs, Tombaugh had found the planet Lowell had been looking for. Though he discovered Pluto's location, Tombaugh did not name it. An eleven-year-old English girl suggested that this new planet be named Pluto after the Roman god of the underworld. The name also honors Lowell since the first two letters of Pluto are Lowell's initials.

Pluto is very small and very far away; yet in the late 1900s, astronomers discovered a satellite, or moon, circling it. That moon, named Charon, is almost the same size as Pluto. Since then, astronomers have discovered other moons too.

For many years, Pluto was classified as the ninth planet in the solar system, but in 2006, it lost its status as a planet and was reclassified as a dwarf planet. Astronomers remain interested in studying Pluto. In fact, NASA sent their New Horizons spacecraft to visit Pluto, and it will reach the dwarf planet in 2015. The spacecraft will take the first close-up pictures of Pluto's surface. Scientists are hoping these pictures will reveal more information about this dwarf planet.

The Tale of the Silent Cheetah

by Dave Bronski

Endings -s, -ed, -ing

accusing	observed	searching
approached	passing	sleeping
carrying	realized	stalked
chased	recognized	stays
failed	resting	taking
gathered	returned	undoing
hunting	roared	watched
keeps	robbing	watching
laughing	running	wondered
lounged		

At day's end, Cheetah always lazily lounged in a tree, resting after a day spent hunting. He often lay awake watching the nighttime activity on the grasslands. One night, Cheetah observed a shadowy figure passing below his tree. He watched as the figure approached the lion sleeping in the grass. Soon the figure was running away, laughing loudly, and carrying the lion's mane. Cheetah recognized the laugh as that of Hyena.

The next morning, Lion roared with anger when he realized his mane was gone. Lion began searching for his mane, but could not find it. Lion stalked through the high grasses, accusing everyone of taking his mane. Lion never approached Cheetah, so Cheetah did not reveal what he had observed.

The next night, Hyena returned to the grasslands, this time taking Zebra's black stripes. Once again, Cheetah failed to tell what he had observed. Night after night, the animals of the grasslands had something taken from them. They wondered who was robbing them of their beautiful manes, stripes, spots, and tails. Yet Cheetah said nothing.

One night, Cheetah fell into a deep sleep. While he was sleeping, Hyena came and took Cheetah's sleeping tree. Cheetah woke up and saw all of the animals' possessions. He quickly gathered them up and returned them. He told the animals about Hyena, and they all chased Hyena away. The grasslands once again became a peaceful, safe home for the animals. Even to this day, Cheetah keeps watch to make sure Hyena stays away.

Helping Burn Victims Heal

by Luca Terrinta

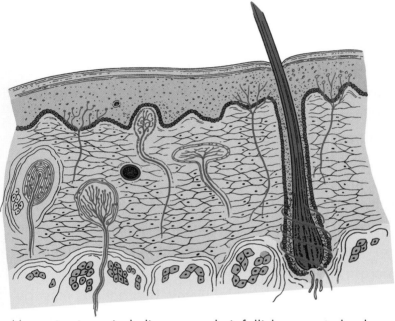

Many structures, including nerves, hair follicles, sweat glands, and blood vessels, are in the three layers of skin.

Shades of Meaning

artificial, man-made	create, forms, generate, produce	framework, structure
at-risk/ defenseless/in danger	defend/protect	heal, mend
	enemies, invaders	keeps, prevents
		urgent, serious

97

If you have ever gotten too close to a flame or touched something very hot, you know how painful a burn can be. Burns may be caused by flame, chemicals, steam, hot liquids, and even electricity. Every year, many thousands of Americans are burned so badly that they lose part of their skin.

Burned skin is a serious problem because our skin protects us. It is made up of two layers. The outer layer, which we see, is thin. Beneath this is a thicker inner layer. It contains blood vessels and nerves that allow us to feel.

Skin prevents bacteria, heat and cold, and harmful substances from reaching our organs. It also keeps body fluids in and helps the body stay warm. When the skin can no longer do its jobs, the body is in danger. Doctors know that burn victims have an urgent need for protection. For decades, research scientists and doctors have worked hard to find a way to help burn victims generate new skin.

To save a badly burned victim, two actions must be taken. First, a surgeon must remove the burned skin. Then, the underlying tissues must be protected. Doctors have found ways to produce artificial skin to cover the burn victim's tissues.

To replace skin on burn victims is called *grafting*. This means implanting living material during an operation. To be successful, skin grafts need to be made of cells that are as much like the victim's own cells as possible.

The body has a system to defend itself from harmful "invaders." If the body senses strange cells, it treats them as enemies and attacks. Doctors know how to "turn off" this system so the body will not reject a transplant. However, turning off the defense system of a burn patient is very dangerous. Bacteria and germs can easily enter the defenseless body and infect the patient. It is easy to see why the best material for a skin graft is the victim's own skin.

How can this be done? Medical scientists have learned how to grow skin cells in a laboratory. They can take healthy skin cells from a patient and use them to grow more cells. The new skin that results can replace the patient's outer layer of skin. The body accepts these cells, for it recognizes them as its own.

A burn unit nurse comforts a patient.

However, for deep burns, both the outer and inner layers of skin must be replaced. In this case, doctors may use artificial skin. This man-made material protects the body and gives a framework on which new skin forms.

Artificial skin has two layers. On the inner layer is a structure made of protein fibers and sticky molecules. It is attached to a smooth, flexible sheet that acts like the skin's outer layer. Over the next few weeks, the patient's own cells create a new inner layer on the framework. Then the upper layer is removed and replaced with a thin layer of the patient's skin cells. Over time, these cells build a new outer layer of skin.

Because burn patients are at-risk while they heal, doctors want them to mend fast. One method to speed recovery involves the use of oxygen under pressure. The patient is placed in a chamber of pure oxygen. The pressure is increased to twice the pressure of the normal atmosphere. These conditions drive ten times the normal amount of oxygen into the blood and cells. Additional oxygen seems to help patients form new blood vessels faster. It also improves blood flow to organs and makes the body's defenses work better.

Today, more burn patients than ever are being healed. The process can take many weeks, though. In the future, scientists will learn even better, faster ways of creating new cells. That will save more lives and lift victims out of pain and danger more quickly.

Down by the River

by Paolo Menendez

Shades of Meaning

canine, dog	garbage, rubbish, trash	looking at, observing, poring over
cast-offs, remnants	grim, serious	thoughtless, unintentional
damaged, destroyed, ruined	label, name	

Jaime loved nothing better than spending a leisurely afternoon at Deer Run River. He'd take fishing gear and his dog Sir Sniffs, a lively boxer, and amuse himself catching and releasing fish and observing the plants and animals around him. Right now Sniffs was living up to his name, running in circles, nose to the ground. The morning, a sunny one in mid-June, was perfect. But Jaime froze on the riverbank, stunned by the grim scene he saw.

The usually inviting green riverbanks and clear water had been destroyed by a storm of pollution; he was looking at garbage and assorted remnants of building materials. Jaime knew that only humans had earned the label Polluters. Thoughtless people sabotaged waterways and oceans with their cast-offs and slowly made them unlivable.

"Careless people!" he shouted angrily. Pollution struck Jaime as the most easily preventable serious problem people faced.

As far as Jaime was concerned, his favorite retreat was ruined. How could this have happened? He pored over the area for clues while his canine partner sniffed a soggy pile of insulation and sneezed. Sandwich wrappers, drink bottles, insulation, a hardhat, and paint rags—Jaime figured out what had happened.

The thunderstorm a few days back had blown this rubbish and any loose materials from the construction site half a mile north, where a big building was going up. It was a relief to think that this damage was unintentional and easily remedied.

Jaime whistled for Sir Sniffs and headed home. He had some phone calls to make and garbage bags to gather. The cleanup of Deer Run River could begin.

Daisy the Dinosaur

By Olivia Takashi

Shades of Meaning

ancient, prehistoric	example, illustration	fossil, remains
dig up, unearthed	figured out, realized	species, type

Sharp eyes and a curious mind can lead to important discoveries. The experience of Daisy Morris gives one illustration of this fact.

In 2008, four-year-old Daisy Morris was walking on the beach with her family. The beach is near her home on the Isle of Wight in Great Britain. Since she was three, Daisy had been interested in fossil hunting.

The girl noticed some small black objects poking out of the sand and decided to dig them up for a closer look. What she discovered was the remains of a strange-looking animal. Its bones were preserved as fossils. Since being turned to stone keeps these remains intact a long time, many fossils are ancient.

Her family took the remains to a fossil expert. After he inspected them, he realized that he "was looking at something very special." Then a team of experts studied the bones. They figured out that the fossil was once part of a small flying reptile called a pterosaur.

Experts believe the dinosaur lived over 100 million years ago. Even more special, this prehistoric reptile was a type completely unknown before 2009. Daisy's find gave us the first example of this species.

Things buried on a beach are usually washed to sea. Without Daisy's action, this animal might have remained hidden forever. Scientists are grateful for Daisy's interest.

They nicknamed the creature "the Dragon from the Isle of Wight." In 2013, fossil experts presented the discovery to the world. They also announced its official name: *Veclidraco daisy morrisae,* in honor of the girl who unearthed it.

The Alarm

by Caleigh Arend

Greek and Latin Roots

dejected	objections	telepathy
insisted	protested	telephone
interrupting	reject	television
object	signal	testify

The sun was up at last, and Priscilla lay on the bed with her muzzle on her forepaws. Her stomach growled as she focused on the three numbers in the clock on the dresser near the telephone. Before long the clock would ring—the breakfast signal! Her best friend would wake up and feed her.

Now she saw the numbers changed. It was finally seven o'clock, but no ring! "Camilla, what do you suppose is wrong?" Priscilla asked the Persian cat lounging on the windowsill.

Camilla stretched in a sunbeam poking through the shutters. "Put your ears back down, Pris," she said, "and don't look so dejected. If you and Leroy weren't so greedy, your food could be left out, just as mine is."

"I object to your calling me greedy, Camilla. I'm a toy greyhound. If you ran 25 miles an hour instead of reclining on the furniture all day, you'd be hungry too. Of course, I can't testify for Leroy."

"Well, I object to your accusing me of being lazy, Miss Pris." Both were concerned, however, that the clock still had not rung.

"Camilla, please jump up on the dresser and pry those shutters all the way open. Maybe the sun will wake her up."

It didn't work. "Why not start howling, which dogs are so good at!" giggled Camilla.

"I object to your attitude! Why should I get scolded for barking in the morning!"

"OK, enough with the objections! Let's go downstairs and see what ideas Leroy has." Camilla and Priscilla ran down the long staircase, and there, next to the television, they found the big basset hound, atop his overstuffed pillow.

"Wake him up by purring," said Priscilla. "He likes that."

It didn't work, so Priscilla stuck her long nose under Leroy's long ear and insisted, "Leroy, PLEASE wake up."

Leroy asked while half awake, "Why are you interrupting my sleep? What's up?" Then he shook his head, and Pris backed away.

Camilla jumped up onto the counter to munch kibble from her bowl, left safely there. "Why do you torment Priscilla, Camilla, when you know she is starving!"

"I reject your criticism, Leroy," replied Camilla. "If you care so much, get up and do something!"

"I don't know why I have to be the one to wake her," he said, hauling his long, lumbering body slowly up the stairs as the Pris and Camilla scampered past.

Now all three watched their best friend. "Telepathy isn't going to work," Camilla quipped.

So Leroy used his huge, padded feet to raise himself to the mattress, face-to-face with his best friend. "Woof!" he called softly, but there was no change. "Woof!" he called again, louder, but with no better luck.

With a third, bold "WOOF!," she flew out of bed.

"I object!" she protested. But no one was there to listen—just three pets exiting hastily through the door.

A Pirate's Wreck

by Alex Jamison

Greek and Latin Roots

aquatic	compare	legend
benefiting	credit	monarchy
claimed	fascinate	proclaim
clamoring	incredible	

Captain William Kidd's life was as incredible as his legend. Questions surrounding him and his lost treasure still fascinate people today. Some stories proclaim him as one of the most colorful pirates of all time. But some people don't compare him to a pirate at all.

Born in Scotland over 350 years ago, Kidd most likely went to sea as a boy. By the late 1600s, he was sailing his own ship for the British monarchy. Most people say he had a change of heart and declared himself a pirate around 1697. Then he claimed as his own the treasure-laden *Cara Merchant.*

Even if Kidd wasn't a pirate, the ship brought him no luck. In about two years, to his credit, Kidd left his ship to try to clear his name. The British, clamoring for justice, tried and hanged him for piracy. Kidd's fate was sealed, but the *Cara Merchant's* fate remained unknown for years.

Two hundred years after Kidd's death, American author Edgar Allen Poe was inspired by the story of Kidd and his treasure to publish the story "The Gold Bug." The main character uses a bug and decodes secret writing to uncover Kidd's lost treasure.

Kidd's legend grows even today. In 2007 the remains of an old ship were found off an island near the Dominican Republic. Its cannons and anchors were still intact, in just ten feet of water. It was the *Cara Merchant!*

Today the ship is an aquatic museum benefiting divers, snorkelers, and historians who seek a glimpse into the life of the real Captain Kidd.

One Woman's High Jump

by Tori MacArthur

> **Greek and Latin Roots**
>
> | | | |
> |---|---|---|
> | athlete(s) | equality | respect |
> | athletic | logic | spectators |
> | dynamic | prologue | unequal |
> | equal | prospects | |

Alice Coachman's career in athletics seemed hopeless at first. However, she earned the respect of athletes all over the world.

Alice was born in a little Georgia town in 1923, almost 100 years ago. Her prospects for success in sports had real challenges. America was segregated. She was an African American and a girl, living in an unequal world. Her father was afraid sports might put her in scary situations because of her gender and race. But a teacher and an aunt helped Alice and her parents see the logic of her participating in sports.

There were no training facilities Alice could use. So she ran and later trained on dirt roads and up and down nearby hills. She built great strength and stamina that way.

Alice thrilled her fans starting in high school. She was powerful in high jump, track, and basketball. Was this a prologue for winning Olympic gold? Would this dynamic athlete prove her equality in front of the whole world?

Then World War II started. The 1940 and 1944 Olympics were not held. So Alice had only one chance, the 1948 Olympic Games in London.

At age 25 and with back problems, Alice showed the world. In front of 83,000 spectators, she set an Olympic high jump record to win gold. She was the first black female of any nation to do so.

Between 1939 and 1948, Alice Coachman won 10 straight high jump championships. She also won 25 indoor and outdoor track events. She would be inducted into nine halls of fame, including the Olympic Hall of Fame in 2004. She had proven herself more than equal to her task!

Whale Watching

by Trevor Sturn

Suffixes -*tion*, -*ion*

communication	intention	motion(s)
ejection	introduction	production
eruption	location	vacation
fascination		

December through early May is whale-watching season in Hawaii. This is the time when humpback whales that migrated from Alaska enjoy the warm waters around Hawaii. It is the time when calves are born and swim with their mothers.

My family has always taken the time to watch the whales each year, so I have been watching whales for over twenty years. When I was young, we usually watched from a beach near our home. We used binoculars and telescopes to watch with fascination as these creatures enjoyed the warm Hawaiian waters.

Then one year the family decided to go to Puukohola Heiau National Historic Site on the Big Island. That's what we call the Island of Hawaii where I live. Our intention was to visit the historic structures at the site, including the heiau, or restored temple, and then sit and watch the whales. Our first stop at the site was the visitor center. There videos and displays provided an introduction to the site and its history. After touring the site, the family settled down to view the whales in the sea. Puukohola means "Hill of the whale," and the site provides an excellent view of whales.

If you have never seen whales breaching, or breaking through the water, you can't imagine what a fantastic experience it is. The whales break the surface and spout out water from their blowholes. The ejection of water from the spouts is something to see. The water may shoot up fifteen feet into the air. The humpbacks also slap their flukes, or tails. The slapping motion as the tail hits the water produces a very loud noise.

The production of sounds and motions may be the whales' means of communication. Whales are known for their singing, but the purpose of the singing is not certain. Some suggest that humpbacks sing to identify the location of other whales. The humpbacks also do pec slaps. A whale does a pec slap by dropping a pectoral fin on one side of its body into the water. Pec slapping and fluke slapping may be the whale's way of letting others know it is in the area.

This year, my friend Don and I took our kayaks to Maui and paddled into the waters where the humpbacks swim. We knew not to get too close. There are rules to protect the whales, and one of them is to stay at least a football field away from the whales.

We paddled away from shore and soon found what we were looking for. Off in the distance were whales playing on the surface of the water. We sat in the calm waters watching them for about fifteen minutes. Both Don and I snapped photographs.

Suddenly there was an eruption as a whale burst out of the water, cleared its blowhole, and slapped its flukes. We captured the sight with our cameras.

This trip to Maui was a fun whale-watching vacation, but soon studying whales will be my career. I'm planning to become a marine scientist and to concentrate my studies on whales. I want to increase our understanding of these magnificent animals. After all I live in the perfect location to study whales!

Arthur Ashe, Tennis Champion

by Malia Sampton

Suffixes -*tion*, -*ion*

association	education	oppression
attention	graduation	promotion
discrimination	instruction	recognition
distinction	introduction	

Arthur Ashe was an American tennis champion who used his talents to win tournaments and to promote the education of young people. Ashe began playing tennis as a young child and proved to be a talented player.

After his graduation from high school, Ashe attended college on a tennis scholarship. There he gained recognition as an excellent player who helped his team win the National Collegiate Athletic Association (NCAA) championship in 1965.

In 1968 Ashe became the first African American to win the men's title in the U.S. Open. Then in 1975, he became the first black man to win at Wimbledon in England. He also had the distinction of being ranked as the world's top player in 1975.

Ashe faced discrimination when he was denied a visa to play in South Africa. He tried to get the country expelled from the international tennis circuit for its racial policies. He wanted the world to be aware of the oppression blacks faced there.

Ashe also developed programs for children. Through the introduction of tennis instruction, the programs were designed to help young people build self-esteem and discipline. The goal of the programs was not only the promotion of tennis. It also focused attention on the importance of education.

Arthur Ashe proved to be a champion on the tennis court. More importantly, however, he was a model of excellence both on and off the tennis court.

American Buffalo

by Dan Owen

Suffixes -*tion*, -*ion*

construction	extinction	protection
elimination	locations	reduction
estimations	population	vacation

Large herds of bison, or American buffalo, once roamed throughout much of North America. Estimations of the number of bison vary. At one time, however, the bison population in North America may have been more than 50 million animals.

Native Americans used bison as a main source of food. They made clothing and coverings from the hides. They also used the hides in the construction of tepees. They used the horns as scoops and spoons. The Native Americans used this valuable resource wisely.

Other Americans did not have the same respect for the animal. In the late 1800s, the reduction of bison herds was swift and nearly complete. Bison became the target of settlers and American hunters. The bison soon were near extinction. It became clear bison needed protection. Game laws were passed and refuges were set up to prevent the elimination of the bison.

Today, some ranchers and farmers are raising bison. There are not many free-roaming bison. National Parks are the locations where most free-roaming bison are found. The largest population of plains bison is in Yellowstone National Park. If you have the opportunity to go on vacation in the park, you are likely to see some of these magnificent creatures.

Curiosity and the Tree

by Janine Torrenti

These boojum trees and other plants are growing in Baja California, Mexico.

Suffix -ous

beauteous	enormous	marvelous
coniferous	fabulous	precious
conspicuous	indigenous	wondrous
curious		

Many people are curious about nature including its wonderful trees. These treasures of nature live almost everywhere and can even inspire people's imaginations.

The boojum tree is one of nature's growing treasures. Found only in Mexico, it looks like an upside-down carrot with spiny twigs. The boojum tree can grow up to five stories tall—that's one huge carrot! Yellowish flowers hang from this tree. Since the base of its trunk is often hollow, it makes a marvelous home for honeybees, so honey lovers like these trees!

Travelers in southeastern Africa might find an important use for the traveler's tree. This tree has a thin trunk that is about three stories tall and is topped with what looks like an enormous fan. The base of each leaf in the fan is shaped like a huge cup. Each cup can hold about a quart of rainwater. In emergencies people can drink precious rainwater that accumulates there.

In India the talipot palm may live for up to 75 years, but it will flower and make fruit only once before dying. Huge branches of beauteous white blooms tower about sixteen feet above its fan-shaped leaves at the top of the trunk. The talipot palm's trunk may be up to eight stories tall and four feet around.

Seychelles, a little island nation in the Indian Ocean, is near India. That is where the double coconut lives. The fruit of the double coconut takes ten years to ripen, and no wonder. Each conspicuous "piece" of fruit can weigh up to 66 pounds.

In South America, Chile is home to a coniferous evergreen called the monkey puzzle tree, which is sacred to the indigenous people. A Spanish explorer was the first European to see this tree over 200 years ago. Later the governor of Chile served its seeds as dessert to an English plant collector. The English visitor went home with five healthy plants. One of them was still alive a hundred years later.

The monkey puzzle tree is also called the Chile pine.

The monkey puzzle tree may look frightening to some. Its shiny, dark green leaves are spiny and hard. Because of the tree's appearance, people thought even monkeys would have trouble figuring out how to climb the sharp spines on its branches. As a result, they gave the tree the name monkey puzzle tree.

Perhaps the most fabulous of all trees are the redwoods growing in the fog belt along the California and Oregon coasts in the United States. Coast redwoods are the tallest living trees. Their trunks can be twenty feet around, and they can grow as high as a thirty-five story building. These trees take 400 to 500 years to mature. Some are more than 1,500 years old—incredible!

Then there is the apple tree. Most people have heard of Johnny Appleseed, a legendary character in books and films. But many people don't know that he was a real person named John Chapman. John lived in New England over 200 years ago.

John honored the animals and plants in nature. He set out in a canoe to plant apple tree orchards wherever he went. The trees were meant to provide food for settlers going West. He would give farmers a tree or two to plant. He accepted payment but never required it. One apple orchard John planted in Ohio still grows today and makes fruit. John knew, so long ago, just how important and wondrous trees can be.

Whistles, Bells, and Steamboats

by Jeff Wheaton

Suffix -ous

cautious	serious
dangerous	grievous
ingenious	

At one time, over a thousand steamboats traveled up and down the Mississippi River. The pilots and other crew had to be cautious to avoid accidents. Boats had ways of communicating to help them navigate and to keep out of dangerous situations. One method was the ingenious use of the steamboats' whistles and bells.

Pilots usually used foot pedals to blast their steam whistles. When two boats approached each other, the pilot going upstream might give one whistle blast. This meant "Go to your right." Two blasts meant "Go to your left." The pilot coming downstream had the choice. If the pilot agreed, he'd whistle once for yes. Five short whistles meant no, followed shortly by two more whistles. The pilot coming toward him would confirm by whistling twice.

In other situations five short whistles could mean a *call to quarters*, or "There's a fire or serious accident here." Five long whistles meant "We are in grievous distress."

Steamboats whistled whenever they landed. If a company had more than one steamboat, they all used the same combination of landing whistles, such as two long and two short; three long and one short; and two long, a short, and a long whistle. In navigation, one tap on the big bell on the roof let sailors know to *sound*, or measure, the water's depth off the right side. Two meant to measure the depth off the left. One more meant to stop measuring.

When a steamboat left a landing, three taps meant it was nearly ready to go. When the engineer blew three times on the small ready whistle atop the boilers, it was time to leave. Signaling with whistles and bells helped the pilots and crews of steamboats communicate on the river.

It's Sticky Stuff

by Ted Foster

Suffix -ous

curious	nervous
enormous	obvious
hilarious	

"Look, Jimmie," Wilbur said, operating his remote-controlled model car. Jimmie was intrigued, especially when it ran into the wall and a wheel fell off. Jimmie thought that was hilarious.

"Watch out, Wilbur," Alva said. "Take that outside, and don't make Jimmie curious about things he can't have. Those remote-controlled toys aren't for small children like Jimmie. You and your friends can play with it, but not in the house."

Wilbur picked up the car and looked for the craft glue in a kitchen cupboard. He glued the wheel back on, put the car and the glue on the table, and went outdoors.

Later that morning, Wilbur returned to the kitchen and discovered an unpleasant surprise. He had left the car and the glue on the kitchen table, and Jimmie had squeezed some glue out on himself, even getting it in his hair. Wilbur asked Alva what they could do. "We can wash it off his hands, but we'll never get it out of his hair," said Alva with a nervous laugh."

Alva looked at Jimmie's curls and wondered what they could possibly do. "Let's go show him to Nona. She'll know what to do."

Just as Alva picked Jimmie up, Nona walked into the room and stopped when she saw Jimmie. "It's obvious," she said smiling. "You have enormous luck, kids, because today is Jimmie's first haircut! Let's put the glue back up in the cupboard."

Garden Fun

by Rose Carlisle

Compound Words

backyard	honeybees	rainfall
blackberries	indoor	sunflowers
blueberries	ladybugs	watermelons
everyone	outdoors	

Having a garden is fun for almost everyone. You can grow one on your patio or in your backyard. There are also community gardens where each person or family plants a small section. Some people have indoor gardens that they grow in large pots. You don't even need soil to grow a garden. One method uses water and nutrients, but no soil. Plants grown in water gardens grow faster and are usually healthier than those grown in soil. No matter what you prefer, you can always enjoy a garden!

A big part of the fun of gardening is deciding which plants you will grow. Part of this decision depends on the size of your garden. If you have a small area, you should choose a few plants that don't need much room. Also, pots hung from a hook will increase your garden space and allow you to grow more plants. If you have a large area, you might choose to grow a variety of plants, including bushes or trees. Another part of your decision of what to grow depends on where your garden is located. If your garden is outdoors, do research about which types of plants will survive and flourish where you live. Take into consideration your growing season and your climate. Most packages of seeds show where the seeds will grow best. You can also find out what will grow well by reading about gardens or asking others who have gardens.

How do you decide which types of plants you will grow? Some people decide to plant only flowers, such as roses, tulips, and sunflowers. Other people like to grow fruits and vegetables, such as tomatoes, carrots, beans, cantaloupe, and watermelons. Fruits that grow on bushes include blackberries, blueberries, and currants. You might even plant a tree that grows apples, oranges, peaches, or avocados.

Before you plant your garden, you will need certain tools. Of course, you will need a shovel! Some people find that a small rake or a trowel (a small hand tool shaped like a shovel) is useful to work the soil. Gloves are important to protect your hands from rocks and thorns. To make sure your plants have water, you will also need a hose or watering can. A small bucket can be used to catch rainfall for later watering or to carry clippings and weeds. Another useful item is a pruning tool to trim plants.

After you plant your garden, you're ready to watch it grow! As your plants grow, they will need care from you. Make sure each plant has enough room to grow. Get rid of any weeds by pulling them. Water your plants if the soil gets too dry. Also, you might want to add special plant food or fertilizer. While you work, look for special, helpful garden friends, such as ladybugs, beetles, and honeybees. These insects are good for your plants, as they help get rid of harmful pests.

Once your plants are grown, sit back and enjoy the results of your work. If you grew flowers, display them in a fancy vase or give some to a friend or a relative. If you grew food, make a tasty snack or meal with your garden treats. Using what you grow is the most rewarding part of garden fun!

Crazy Apple Salad

by Kyle Jackson

Compound Words

afternoon	cookout	something
anyone	foolproof	supermarket
cannot	homemade	teaspoon

A salad is something anyone can make and enjoy. It is a nice homemade treat, not only to have with meals but also to present at a party, picnic, or cookout. Here is a special type of salad that is tasty and colorful. The fancy name for this salad is Waldorf Salad, but you might just call it the Crazy Apple Salad!

What makes this salad crazy? Well, it doesn't have the usual ingredients that are found in what people think of as a regular salad. It doesn't have lettuce, tomatoes, carrots, or cucumbers. Instead, this salad is primarily made of fruit. It's so easy to prepare that it's foolproof, doesn't require any special tools or skills, and can be made quickly in an afternoon. All of the ingredients are readily found at a supermarket or other grocery store.

So how is this Crazy Apple Salad made? First assemble and prepare the ingredients with the help of an adult. Chop $1\frac{1}{2}$ cups of cranberries and then chop two unpeeled red apples. Measure one cup of seedless green grapes and cut each grape in half. Finally, prepare one cup of small, chopped celery pieces. Measure $\frac{1}{3}$ cup of raisins and $\frac{1}{4}$ cup of walnut pieces, and stir all the prepared ingredients together. In a separate bowl, combine $\frac{1}{4}$ teaspoon of cinnamon with 8 ounces of vanilla yogurt and blend them together. Toss this yogurt dressing with the rest of the ingredients, put the salad in a bowl, and decorate with additional walnut pieces. For best results, make sure your salad is chilled before it is served.

For a simple, delightful, and colorful salad, this one cannot be beat!

The Surprise Visitor

by Elena Reyes

Compound Words

airplanes	necklace	tiptoe
airport	someone	underground
Grandmother	suitcase	weekend
highway	sunglasses	

Alicia woke up one summer day to the sound of her mother vacuuming the carpet. Usually the two of them worked together on the weekend to clean their apartment. Wondering why her mother was cleaning this morning, Alicia walked into the room. Her mother smiled at her and told her to put on some cute clothes and her favorite necklace. Mother also told her to wear her new sandals and put a nice ribbon in her hair. Then she winked and told Alicia she was in for a big surprise.

Alicia got dressed and brushed her hair, remembering to tie it back with the ribbon. By the time she was finished, her mother was ready to leave. Mother put on her sunglasses and they drove off in the car. After a few minutes, Mother got on the highway and drove for a long time. Finally she turned off at the airport.

Mother parked the car in the underground lot. She wrote down where they parked, and she and Alicia began the long walk to the terminal. Alicia looked at the people there and wondered where the airplanes would take these strangers. Suddenly her mother called Alicia's name and pointed to someone in the crowd. Alicia stood on tiptoe to see over the adults and strained to see the lady with the suitcase who was walking toward them. It was Grandmother, coming to visit them! Alicia beamed when she saw her, gave her a kiss, and took her hand. Alicia was definitely surprised and also very happy. Three generations of the family were together on this wonderful day.

Paul and Other Octopuses

by Nita Murphy

Carla and Tess were fascinated by the octopus swimming in its tank. Everyone had thought the visit to the aquarium would be fun, but this was better than anyone had imagined.

"The placard on this tank," said Carla, "tells us that the octopus belongs to the genus Octopus, which is a large group of cephalopods living in shallow water. All octopuses have eight arms. **Octo** means 'eight' and *cephalo* means 'head.'"

"Some can be very small," added Tess, recalling some information the class had previewed before coming to the aquarium.

"Yes," Carla continued, returning to the information on the placard, "they go from about two inches to almost thirty feet! The octopus lays 100,000 eggs at a time! It uses camouflage for protection, and it can change colors very quickly. This particular species is said to be the most intelligent of all invertebrates."

"What is an *invertebrate*?" Tess inquired.

"Here it says it's an animal without a backbone.

"This particular octopus doesn't appear to be a very smart invertebrate."

"Well, it is a highly intelligent sea creature. In the sea, octopuses in its species dig up coconut shells and carry them along as protective shelters. Scientists say the octopuses are using the coconut shells as tools, showing they are intelligent animals."

"I recall hearing about an octopus named Paul," Mo said, walking up to the girls. "Do you ever watch the World Cup?"

"Sure, it's the international soccer competition," Carla answered.

"Well, there was an octopus named Paul in West Germany that amazed the world by correctly predicting the winners of all seven of Germany's World Cup games in South Africa in 2010. It also correctly predetermined the winner of the final game."

"How did people react to Paul's achievements," Tess asked. "Did they acknowledge his achievements in some way?"

"You bet!" Mo said. "Paul inspired a special clothing line and smart phone applications, and a video was made about him."

Paul correctly predicted that Spain would win the 2010 World Cup in soccer.

"How did he preselect the winners?"

"His caretakers attached the national flags of teams playing each other to boxes of mussels. Octopuses eat mussels, crabs, lobsters, and other mollusks. When they put the boxes in Paul's tank, he drifted toward the food, and they just waited to see which box he opened first."

"Whatever became of Paul?"

"He died when he was two and a half."

"Did people do anything special?"

"Yes! Sea Life Centre in Oberhausen, Germany, reproduced his image in a memorial. He is shown on top of a soccer ball. In the middle is a see-through window where there's a jar containing his ashes."

"I wonder whether other octopuses can tell future events," Carla said.

"I don't know, but if there are others, it's a good idea to find them. Donations were made in Paul's name that helped pay for a permanent sea turtle center in Greece."

"Say, isn't the plural of octopus actually octopi, not octopuses?" asked Tess.

"I don't know, but maybe we should ask the guy in this tank," Mo said.

"Sure! I have an idea," Carla said. "Tess, you say 'octopi' and Mo, you say 'octopuses.' See which of you he drifts toward.

"But let me prewarn you. We'll have to check a dictionary too."

Ötzi the Cook

By Elena Novak

Prefixes *pre-, re-*

prehistoric	recreated	removed
predated	reenacts	researchers
reanalyzed		

Before people learned to write, they had learned to cook. In fact, it's likely that brain development in prehistoric people was greatly enhanced with cooked food. Eating cooked food significantly increased people's intake of nutrients. It also helped them avoid diseases they could contract from raw meat.

Open cooking fires predated other methods. These fires were built in wind-protected, shallow pits. Plant leaves and grass were used as fuel. Rocks and stones were included to hold the heat. Once pottery was invented, cooking became much easier. Liquids could be boiled, so people could make stews and soups.

Evidence uncovered by researchers shows that prehistoric people ate meat, fish, shellfish, vegetables, grains, nuts, insects, and fruits. They knew how to roast, boil, smoke, and dry foods. Archaeologists have recreated prehistoric meals such as wild boar kabobs, fish stew, meat pudding, and pancakes.

Prehistoric people left incredible cave paintings such as those in the Cave of the Spider in eastern Spain. One drawing shows a person with a shoulder basket or gourd hanging on three thin vines, picking up honeycombs. Another reenacts a goat hunt using bows and arrows.

Ötzi the Iceman may give us the best clues to early food. The frozen body of this early hunter was removed from a glacier in Italy. Scientists analyzed and reanalyzed everything about Ötzi. They found that his stomach contained partly digested grain, herbs, red deer, and ibex. Charcoal particles indicated that for one of Ötzi's last meals, he barbecued.

Pets and the President

By Sean Ryker

Prefixes *pre-*, *re-*

precaution	prewarned	renewed
preoccupied	reassuring	restarted

Abraham Lincoln, the sixteenth president, loved animals. He cared for them even when he was busy and preoccupied. He could play with cats for hours. His wife Mary Todd Lincoln said "Cats" when she was asked if he had any hobbies.

Once when traveling, Lincoln saved three orphaned kittens. Before he restarted his trip, he found them a good home.

When Lincoln was elected president, he lived in Illinois and was the proud owner of Fido, a mixed-breed dog. Fido was terrified by the fireworks celebrating Mr. Lincoln's election in 1860. The Lincolns were concerned about Fido's health, so as a precaution they decided to leave Fido at home. They would not take him to Washington, D.C. They knew the long train trip and city noises would scare him. They enlisted two boys from the neighborhood to care for Fido. Lincoln prewarned the boys that Fido scratched the front door to be let into the house. He also was not yelled at for having muddy paws. The Lincolns even gave the boys their sofa. They hoped the familiar sofa would be reassuring to Fido after they left for Washington.

Once the Lincolns were in the White House, it soon became home to rabbits, cats, and goats. Tad and Willie, the Lincolns' sons, liked to hitch the goats to carts and be pulled around by the goats.

Lincolns love of animals extended to a holiday turkey. The turkey was sent to the White House in 1863 for a holiday meal. Tad begged the president to stay the turkey's execution, and he did. The custom of saving a turkey from becoming a holiday dinner has since been renewed by modern-day presidents.

Acknowledgments

Photographs:

1 Associated Press; **3** Layne Kennedy/CORBIS; **9** La Vieja Sirena/Shutterstock; **11** George Dolgikh/Shutterstock; **18** Piotr Malczyk/Shutterstock; **20** David P. Smith/Shutterstock; **25** Michael Nicholson/CORBIS; **27** Bettmann/CORBIS; **34** Daddy Cool/ Fotolia; **35** Elena Elisseeva/Shutterstock; **41** Jorge Salcedo/ Shutterstock; **43** camrocker/Fotolia; **49** Daniel Korzeniewski/ Shutterstock; **51** visceralimage/Shutterstock; **57** Tooga/Getty Images; **59** Andrew Davis Tucker/Newscom; **65** Everett Collection Inc/Alamy; **67** Getty Images; **73** Christie's Images/CORBIS; **75** Ruggiero Scardigno/Fotolia; **81** North Wind Picture Archives/ Alamy; **83** kathy libby/Fotolia; **89** anekoho/Shutterstock; **91** Rechitan Sorin/Shutterstock; **97** Science Source; **99** Steven Widoff/Alamy; **113** Paul Souders/Getty Images; **116** Ron Dahlquist/Getty Images; **121** Tai Power Seeff/Getty Images; **123** Alan Fern/Alamy; **129** Eric Krouse/Shutterstock; **131** prudkov/ Shutterstock; **137** lavigne herve/Shutterstock; **139** AFP/Getty Images.